SEAHORSE

('siːhɔːs,' *Hippocampus*)

Seahorses are found in tropical and temperate waters around the world. There are more than fifty-four known species, ranging in size from ⅕ in to 14 in (1.5 cm to 35.5 cm). Seahorses are the only animal species where the male carries the unborn young, gestating the eggs in their brood pouch. Seahorses move around by using a tiny fin on their back that flutters up to thirty-five times per second.

GREEN SEA TURTLE

('griːn si tərdl,' *Chelonia mydas*)

Green sea turtles are so named because of the color of their fat and cartilage rather than their shells, which are usually brown or olive, and occasionally black. They can grow to more than 3 ft (1 m) in length and inhabit tropical and subtropical waters all over the world. They travel immense distances between their feeding grounds and their hatching beaches, with some turtles swimming more than 1,600 miles (2,600 km).

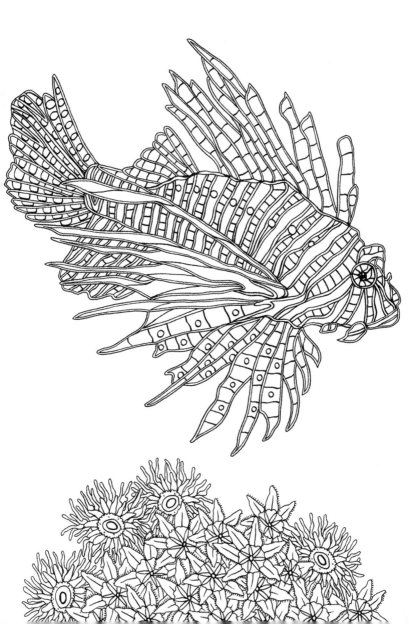

LIONFISH

('lʌɪənfɪʃ,' *Pterois volitans*)

With its unusually long and resplendent fins, the lionfish creates a display around its head and body of dark orange and white stripes, resembling a mane. The equally beautiful fins on its back, however, can deliver a shot of powerful venom, although these are generally used only in self-defense. The lionfish uses its ornate appearance to disguise itself among the coral, waiting to pounce on passing fish and shrimp. Lionfish can grow up to 15 in (40 cm) in length.

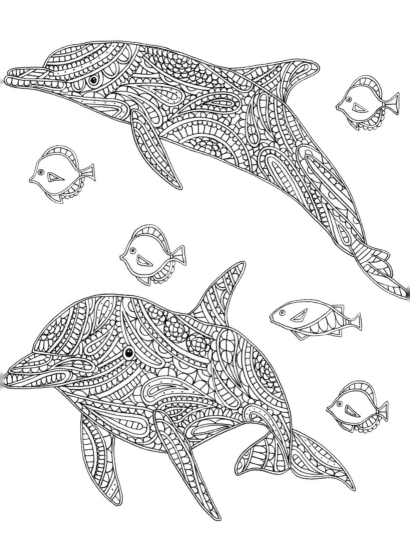

BOTTLENOSE DOLPHIN
('bɒt(ə)lnəʊz dɒlfɪn,' *Tursiops truncatus*)

Naturally sociable by nature, bottlenose dolphins swim in packs called "pods," communicating with each other in a language of whistles, squeaks, and body movements, working as a team to catch their fish. The color of their skin is a camouflage: when viewed from above, the upper body blends with the blue-gray depths of the ocean, while their white bellies, if viewed from below, mimic the white glare of the surface. Bottlenose dolphins can grow as large as 14 ft (4 m) long, and their upturned mouths give the impression of a perpetual smile.

COCONUT OCTOPUS

('kəʊkənʌt ɒktəpəs,' *Amphioctopus marginatus*)

The coconut octopus measures just 6 in (15 cm) in diameter (including its eight legs) and is found in shallow, tropical waters, moving slowly along the sandy bottom, feeding on crabs and shrimp. It is usually a dark orange color with a frill of white suckers that resemble coral. Its soft, velvety body means it's defenseless to attack, so to protect itself it rolls into a ball, winding six legs around its head, and using the remaining two to keep moving. This octopus also cleverly picks up discarded coconut shells to use as protection.

ORIENTAL SWEETLIPS

(ˈɔːrɪˈɛnt(ə) swiːtlɪps,' *Plectorhinchus vittatus*)

Oriental sweetlips are found in the coral reefs of the Indian Ocean. They're part of a species known as "grunts"; fish that make a sound by grinding their teeth plates together and that have oversize rubberlike lips. They're characterized by their unusual spots and stripes: their bodies are adorned with thin black-and-white stripes while their fins are spotted with black polka dots on yellow. Their pattern changes as they age, and young fish are marked with thin stripes on their tails, which then transform into black dots as an adult.

ORANGE CLOWNFISH

(ˈɒrɪn(d)ʒ klaʊnfɪʃ,' *Amphiprion percula*)

Aside from its striking orange-and-white striped body, the clownfish is also famous for its important reciprocal relationship with the anemone. Before making its home among them, it accustoms itself by lightly stroking different parts of its skin on their tentacles. While the anemone offers the clownfish morsels of food and shelter from prey, the clownfish in return repels invaders and grooms the anemone to rid it of parasites. All clownfish are born male, but are able to change sex to female if the only breeding female dies.

DUGONG

(‘duːɡɒŋ,’ *Dugong dugon*)

The dugong (which comes from the Malay, meaning "lady of the sea") is of closer relation to the elephant than any marine mammal. It can grow up to 10 ft long (3 m) and weighs around 926 lb (420 kg). As an herbivore, its habitat is limited to coastal areas with seagrass meadows where it sucks up vegetation with its square-shaped mouth. The dugong is usually a pale white color as a baby, but changes to soft gray, then a deeper gray-blue to brown as an adult.

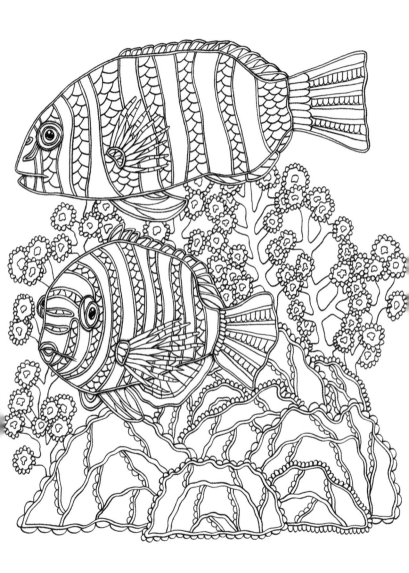

HARLEQUIN TUSKFISH
('hɑːlɪkwɪn tʌskfɪ ʃ,' *Choerodon fasciatus*)

The harlequin tuskfish is found in the coral reefs of the western Pacific Ocean. As its name suggests, it is known for its brilliant multicolored coat of blue, green, and orange. Other distinguishing features are its protruding blue teeth with which it can rip through invertebrates such as crustaceans. The harlequin tuskfish can grow as large as 12 in (30 cm). Younger tuskfish have "false eye spots" (known as *ocelli*) around their fins. The *ocelli* are photosensitive and allow the fish to notice changes of light in their vicinity, which could signal a predator.

LEAFY SEADRAGON

(ˈliːfi siːdrag(ə)n,ˈ *Phycodurus eques*)

The leafy seadragon is part of the same family as the seahorse and its incredible "leafy" shape makes it almost indistinguishable from seaweed or plants such as kelp. It can grow up to 14 in (35 cm) in total, its body consisting of leaflike branches in brown, yellow, and orange. Although it appears to float through the water like a plant, it actually has small fins on the upper and rear body. Leafy seadragons are now approaching endangered species status because their habitat is threatened by pollution.

PACIFIC SEA NETTLE

(‘pə’sɪfɪk siː nɛt(ə)l,’ *Chrysaora fuscescens*)

One of the most stunning jellyfish species, the Pacific sea nettle has a gorgeous yet delicate yellow body with deep red stringlike outer tentacles and beautiful streams of ruffled white inner tentacles that resemble trails of blossom. It uses its tentacles like a net, amassing food as it passes by while delivering a potent sting, which is poisonous but not lethal. These tentacles can grow up to 16 ft (4.8 m) long and they start the digesting process as they pass the food up to the mouth.

BIGFIN REEF SQUID

('bɪgfɪn riːf skwɪd,' *Sepioteuthis lessoniana*)

The bigfin reef squid has oversize eyes, arms with rows of suckers, and a large oval fin that extends around its body. It can vary in color from translucent white to yellow, pink, or violet. Its skin contains light-reflecting cells so that it can quickly change body color and pattern to be able to camouflage itself. It is remarkable for its incredibly quick growth rate, growing to 1.3 lb (600 g) in only four months. However, it also has a very short lifespan of only 315 days. The bigfin reef squid swims in schools and is attracted by light.

KILLER WHALE

('kɪlə weɪl,' *Orcinus orca*)

Able to survive in all climates, the killer whale is found in both the cold Arctic Ocean as well as tropical seas. It can grow up to 30 ft (9 m) long and is known for its rows of incredibly sharp teeth and clever methods of hunting. It eats fish, sharks, turtles, and birds, either herding its prey to the surface and giving it powerful blows with a tail fin, or holding it down so that it suffocates. Killer whales often breach the surface of the ocean, performing jumps and tail slaps to interact, woo, or just play with each other.

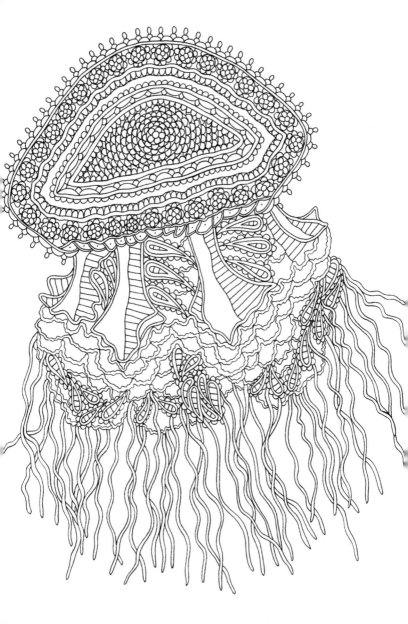

LION'S MANE JELLYFISH

('lʌɪən meɪn dʒɛlɪfɪʃ,' *Cyanea capillata*)

This large species of jellyfish is known for its long, flowing red and yellow manelike tentacles, of which there are more than 800, some even reaching lengths of 120 ft (37 m). The lion's mane jellyfish can vary in color from red or purple to orange. It survives on a diet of plankton, other jellyfish, small fish, and shrimp, which it immobilizes with a sting from its tentacles. It uses pulsations to move slowly through the water and relies on currents to move greater distances.

ATLANTIC MACKEREL

('at'lantık mak(ə)r(ə)l,' *Scomber scombrus*)

Atlantic mackerel typically swim in dense schools of many thousands, creating a beautiful visual effect when seen through the water. The upper body is a darkish green or blue with wavy stripes, and the lower body shimmers with a silvery, brassy iridescence. The mackerel needs a lot of oxygen, so it swims continuously with a swift sideways movement to channel enough water through its gills. Mackerel breed close to the surface because their eggs float, but this also makes them vulnerable to predators.

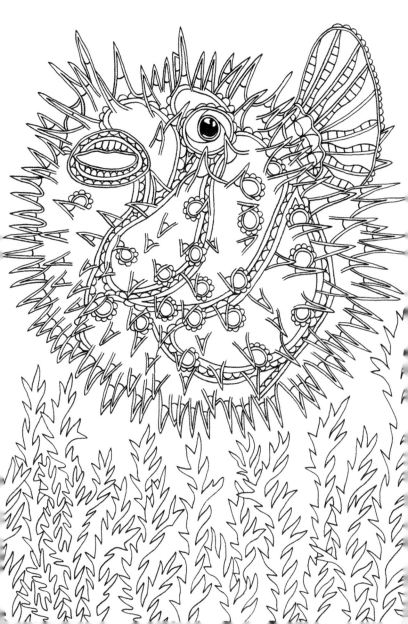

PUFFERFISH
('pʌfəfɪʃ,' *Tetraodontidae*)

The pufferfish, as its name suggests, is known for its ability to inflate itself by quickly ingesting huge amounts of water when under threat. It can't get away from predators quickly, but it is poisonous when eaten, containing a toxin that is foul-tasting to fish and deadly to humans. Some species additionally have sharp spikes that protrude from their skin. They grow up to 2 ft (61 cm) in length and their teeth are molded together to form a hard gum to crush invertebrates.

RACCOON BUTTERFLYFISH
(ˈrəkuːn bʌtəflʌɪfɪ ʃ,ˈ *Chaetodon lunula*)

Like its namesake, the eyes of the raccoon butterflyfish are surrounded by a black-and-white band that resembles a mask. Found in shallow tropical waters, it looks for shelter close to reef beds. It has a beautiful coloration of yellow, red, and gold stripes across its body and dark orange edging in an oval shape around the fins. Some also have a "false eyespot" that confuses predators who are fooled into attacking the tail rather than its face. It lives in cavelike areas and feeds on coral and anemone, growing to 8 in (20 cm) long.

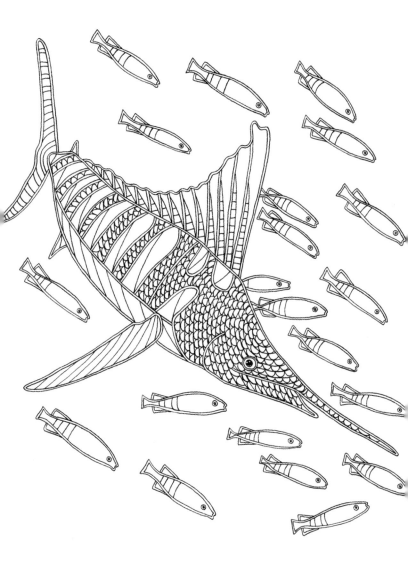

STRIPED MARLIN

('strʌɪpt mɑːlɪn,' *Kajikia audax*)

Known for its long, swordlike beak, the striped marlin is under threat from the fishing industry as it is commercially fished for sushi. It can grow to a maximum length of 14 ft (4.2 m) and reach a weight of 420 lb (190 kg), so is therefore also sought after by sports fishermen. The striped marlin is usually a beautiful blue-gray color, but when courting or feeding, its stripes become electric blue or phosphorescent. Preferring warmer waters, it migrates toward the equator in the cold seasons.

MANDARINFISH

('mand(ə)rɪnfɪʃ,' *Synchiropus splendidus*)

Truly one of the most beautiful fish in the ocean, the mandarinfish has a striking and intricate pattern. The fish are mainly bright blue and orange, but also green, purple, and yellow—they are often described as psychedelic. The mandarinfish is typically shy, and is very small in size, about 2¼ in (6 cm), which can make it even harder to spot. It has a wide, square-shaped head and two leglike fins that are longer than the rest, which gives the impression that it can "walk" when swimming close to the seabed.

NUDIBRANCH

('njuːdɪbraŋk,' *Nudibranchia*)

These marine mollusks, or sea slugs, can survive in both cold and warm waters from the tropics to the Antarctic Ocean. Typically the size of a finger, their soft bodies crawl slowly along the ocean floor or across coral. Their main defense is to ingest toxins in the food they eat, storing and then discharging them as poison when attacked. Some species are noted for their strangely formed bodies with lumpy gills and extraordinarily contrasting color patterns, intended as a visual warning to predators signaling their toxic flesh.